SAMI MULAJ

"BROKEN DREAMS"

Poems

English translation by
Укë Zenel Buçpapaj
"HORARY FELLOW IN WRITING"
THE UNIVERSITY OF IOWA,
IOWA CITY, IOWA, USA, 1992

Prepared for publication by
Kujtim Hajdari

" BROKEN DREAMS "

Author: Sami Mulaj

Edited by Gloria Mindock

Photo cover by Vaka Bler
Durres, Albania

Copyright 2024:
Sami Mulaj

Broken Dreams

OVERVIEW

Written by Ukë ZENEL Buçpapaj

Edited by Gloria Mindock, American poetess and publisher

Sami Mulaj's poetry collection is a masterful exploration of the human experience, blending themes of nostalgia, love, nature, and societal critique. His verses traverse the intimate landscapes of personal memory and collective history, painting vivid images of both beauty and desolation. Through his poignant words, Mulaj captures the human condition, offering readers a window into the soul's deepest longings and reflections.

Themes

Nostalgia and Longing

Mulaj's poetry is suffused with a profound sense of nostalgia and longing, particularly for his homeland. Poems like "The Song of the Emigrant" and "The Mist of Homeland" encapsulate the emotional duality of living between two worlds. These verses poignantly convey the bittersweet essence of being an expatriate, where dreams of the homeland sustain life but also underscore the pain of separation.

Love and Relationships

Love, in its various forms, is a central theme in Mulaj's work. Romantic love, familial bonds, and the complexities of human relationships are explored with depth and sensitivity. Poems such as "I Love You!" and "Eternal Love" delve into the enduring nature of true affection, while "Without a Father" and "Mother's Secret" highlight the irreplaceable bonds within a family, celebrating the enduring impact of these connections.

Nature and Environment
The natural world serves as both a backdrop and a metaphor in Mulaj's poetry. His keen observations and deep appreciation for nature are evident in poems like "Mountain Silence" and "The River of Life." Through these verses, Mulaj draws parallels between natural phenomena and the human journey, emphasizing the interconnectedness of all things and the cyclical nature of life.

Social and Political Commentary
Mulaj does not shy away from addressing the sociopolitical landscape. His poems often critique corruption, injustice, and the impact of historical events on the present. "Thieves of the Homeland" and "The Missing Justice" are poignant commentaries on the failings of societal systems and the enduring quest for justice and truth. These works serve as a call to awareness and action, reflecting Mulaj's commitment to social justice.

Inspirations and Influences
Mulaj's poetry is deeply influenced by his personal experiences as an expatriate, his Albanian heritage, and his observations of societal changes. Historical events, cultural traditions, and the natural beauty of Albania serve as rich sources of inspiration. Additionally, the works of other poets and literary figures have shaped his poetic voice, allowing him to create a unique and resonant body of work.

Broken Dreams

Stylistic Elements

Imagery and Symbolism

Mulaj's poetry is rich with vivid imagery and symbolic language, creating a sensory experience that deeply resonates with readers. The use of natural elements as metaphors for human conditions is a hallmark of his style, bringing his themes to life in a tangible and evocative manner.

Lyricism and Rhythm

The rhythmic quality of Mulaj's verse adds a musicality that enhances the emotional impact of his words. Poems such as "Poets Are Like Stars" and "The Wild Horses of Dreams" demonstrate this lyrical beauty, inviting readers to engage not just intellectually but also emotionally and viscerally.

Bilingual Expression

The inclusion of translations by Ukë Zenel Buçpapaj allows Mulaj's poetry to reach a broader audience while retaining its original Albanian essence. This bilingual approach underscores the universal themes and emotions that transcend linguistic boundaries, highlighting the shared human experience.

Poetic Techniques and Innovations

Mulaj employs a range of poetic techniques to convey his themes and emotions. His use of free verse, coupled with occasional structured forms, allows for a dynamic and flexible expression. The interplay between rhythm and imagery creates a captivating reading experience, drawing readers into the world of his poetry.

Reader Engagement and Impact
Mulaj aims to engage readers on multiple levels—emotionally, intellectually, and aesthetically. His poetry invites readers to reflect on their own experiences and the world around them. By addressing universal themes through a personal lens, Mulaj creates a powerful connection with his audience, encouraging them to explore the depths of their own emotions and thoughts.

Critical Reception and Awards
Mulaj's poetry has garnered acclaim for its emotional depth, vivid imagery, and social relevance. His work has been recognized in various literary circles, earning awards and commendations for its contribution to contemporary Albanian poetry.

Emotional Tone
The emotional tone of Mulaj's poetry ranges from melancholic and reflective to hopeful and uplifting. There is a persistent undercurrent of resilience and a celebration of the enduring human spirit, even in the face of adversity and change. Mulaj's ability to convey deep emotions with authenticity and grace makes his poetry a compelling and enriching read.

Broken Dreams

CONTENT

- OVERVIEW —————————————————3
1. THE BRIDGE OF LOVE ————————————-6
2. THE DELAYED ONE—————————————-7
3. DO NOT————————————————————12
4. THE BIRDS ——————————————————— 13
5. THE TWO QUEENS ——————————————14
6. BROKEN DREAMS ——————————————15
7. WINTER HAS IT'S HONOR TOO———————-16
8. THE RIVER OF LIFE —————————————-18
9. MOON OF MY HOMELAND ——————————19
10. GREED ————————————————————-20
11. TEMPLE OF SILENCE———————————— 21
12. THE SEA OF DREAMS ————————————-23
13. MEMORIES ——————————————————-24
14. YOU ARE BESIDE ME————————————-25
15. LAND OF POETS ———————————————-26
16. THE WHIM OF A CLOUD————————————27
17. A GLOOMY MORNING ————————————-29
18. POETRY EMBRACES YOU——————————-30
19. THE KISS ———————————————————-31
20. THE QUARREL OF THE CLOUDS ——————-32
21. LITTLE BIRD —————————————————-33
22. SEASONS ———————————————————-34
23. THE DREAM OF FREEDOM ——————————-36
24. FRIENDS ———————————————————-37

25. IN LIFE'S SANCTUARY —39
26. NIGHTS —40
27. WHITE SNOW —41
28. WHEN I WAS A BABY —43
29. RAIN —44
30. BIRTHPLACE —45
31. THE FIFTH SEASON —46
32. OUR ANTIQUITY — 48
33. OUR CASTLES — 49
34. THE GRAVE OF THE BORDER — 50
35. MOTHER'S SECRET —52
36. WITHOUT POETS —53
37. THE LAST BITE — 54
38. I DIE FOR YOU —55
39. MY YEARS —56
40. SNOW —58
41. THE FIRST KISS — 60
42. HOPES —61
43. THE SEA OF POETRY —62
44. ETERNAL LOVE — 63
45. ABANDONED OAK — 64
46. ARTISTS —66
47. I WANT TO PUT SLEEP TO SLEEP —67
48. I CARRY MY TEAR EVERYWHERE —68
49. NOW I AM FAR AWAY — 69
50. INSPECTION —71
51. DAYS —72

Broken Dreams

52. DESOLATE FOREST —————————————————73
53. THAT MORNING ——————————————————-74
54. HOW OFTEN ————————————————— 76
55. FAMILY DAY————————————————————-77
56. MY VERSE ——————————————————————78
57. TRAIN STATION ——————————————————— 79
58. NOBODY KNOWS US———————————————— 80
59. THROUGH THE LIGHT OF PAIN ———————————— 81
60. POLAR BEAR————————————————————— —83
61. THE BOSOM OF THE EARTH ——————————————84
62. CONTRAST OF EMIGRANTS ——————————————85
63. THE BIRD'S LAMENT ——————————————————87
64. THE BALLAD OF DEPARTURE ————————————— 88
65. TRINITY—————————————————————————90
66. HANDS ———————————————————————— —-91
67. FORGIVE ME, MY POETRY ——————————————- 92
68. LIFE IS A MOTHER ——————————————————93
69. MY AUNT'S PASSPORT -————————————————94
70. AM I A HOMELAND ——————————————————95
71. MORNING COFFEE MUSIC ——————————————96
72. THE DAM———————————————————————- 97
73. THE SMILE OF TOMORROW ———————————— 98
74. MY STORY ——————————————————————99
75. MOTHERS ————————————————————— 100
76. PARALLELS————————————————————————101
 - SHORT LITERARY BIOGRAPHY—————————————- 102

9

THE BRIDGE OF LOVE

Do not become a bridge—
This saying has lingered since...

But without a bridge,
Love would never exist;
The shores would remain barren,
Like mist without a breeze...

Broken Dreams

THE DELAYED ONE

I want the sky
To be pierced with lead,
For my nation
Is delayed.

Couldn't it
Have delayed the delay?

The delayed one,
They say he will arrive late,
Even at his own funeral.

Couldn't it
Have delayed the delay?

DO NOT

Broken Dreams

Do not
Close my eyes
When I die.

Let my eyes
Kiss
The sky.

Two blues together,
Now with the horizon line,
Faded.

Broken Dreams

THE BIRDS

With feathers they cut through continents,
Flock by flock,
Without tickets or airport checks.

They descend just so,
Dancing in the grain fields,
Celebrating harvest
With full crops.

They do not wait for autumn;
From spring to spring,
They migrate
Without permits or visas,
Traveling
To open spaces.

THE TWO QUEENS

There are two queens:

Mother is the first,
Violet is the second.

Violet, queen
Of flowers and beauty,

Mother, queen
Of hearts and love.

Violet
Brings fragrance and health to the home,
Mother,
To the future...

BROKEN DREAMS

Dreams that are broken
Resemble birds
Competing with airplanes.

The janitor at the airport
Wipes the broken wings
Of some birds...

Broken Dreams
WINTER HAS ITS HONOR TOO

We count every misdeed
Of the harsh winter,
Frost scorching the trees
From above.

Birds flee,
The remaining ones flutter over the snow,
The whiteness dazzles the gaze,
Mountains look forlorn.

It takes an hour from the day
And adds it to the night, treating it gently.

Without winter, autumn would be like a harlot,
Leaving the tree,
Her daughters,
Naked,
Their dresses and nightgowns
Tossed aside, with or without grace.

Winter, like an honorable grandfather,
Covers them with white snow sheets,
Leaving them neither shamed
Nor frozen.

Broken Dreams

He puts the trees to sleep,
So that in spring
They rise like brides,
With soft breasts
And a sweet fragrance.

THE RIVER OF LIFE

It begins as a small stream
Where the horizon
Kisses the sky.

It cools the banks,
Sometimes rushing with force,
Sometimes like a fearless boy,
Leaping from rocks as a waterfall.

In its descent,
On the plain,
Boats anchor,
And ships
Come and go.

At last,
The river disappears
Into the sea,
A thunder subsides,
And there, the line with the horizon
Fades, fades away.

MOON OF MY HOMELAND

To the moon of my homeland
I reveal everything—
Joys,
Sorrows,
Hopes.

The moon here,
In this foreign land,
Shatters my dreams.

Moon of my homeland,
You warm my soul...

GREED

A greedy man,
Though married,
Pursued a beautiful girl.
To others,
He spoke of her
As his lover and friend.
But she
Loved another.

One day, he left this world,
Perhaps burdened by this too,
His soul weighed down with sorrow.

When she heard,
She went to his grave,
Opened her dress,
Bared her thighs,
As if ready,
"Here," she said, "you wretch,
Satisfy yourself now!"

Broken Dreams

TEMPLE OF SILENCE

The old tower
Reminds me of a temple.

The wrinkles on its walls
Like the brows of grandparents…

Somewhere are kept
My scribbles
From when I was a child.

The floor preserves
The footprints of cradles.

Even the ink stains
Spilled by my sister
Are still not erased.

How I wish
The fireplace
Would open its mouth
To tell
Of our forgetfulness.

The rebab,
With a furrowed face,

Broken Dreams

Left its song unfinished…

Silent,
I hear a call—
The tower calls out,
Here,
Children.

My silence
Wants to become
Silence with a mouth…

Broken Dreams

THE SEA OF DREAMS

The tides rock me gently,
Dreams brought by seagulls.

Like on Treasure Island,
I am an undiscovered Robin Hood.

The wings of my memories
Are broken,
And the feathers of my old hopes
Have drifted away.

The footprints of my first love
In the sand, I cannot find.
The post-sunset breeze
Has cast them onto another island.

In those footsteps,
Another Robin Hood has walked...

MEMORIES

I gathered my memories,
Combed them with the teasel of years,
Shook them with the fragrance of seasons.

The sunny ones I released like doves
To soar into the blue.

What remained,
The misty ones,
I sealed in a bottle.

A hundred years from now,
The wave of a glance
Will bring them ashore...

Broken Dreams

YOU ARE BESIDE ME

Like a butterfly on a leaf,
Like a bee on thyme,
Like a murmuring spring,
Like tender dew
When the eye of the day opens,

You are beside me.

LAND OF POETS

My homeland,
Blessed with beauty,
On crest-topped peaks
Breathes poetry into the skies.

Three thousand years ago,
My ancestors,
On clay tablets,
Wrote poetry…
It's said the Babylonians
Learned from my forebears.
When the tablets were lost,
They wrote their names in the skies
And grew their stature
With the heights of the mountains…

The letters transformed into trees,
The trees into traps
For the wicked enemy…

THE WHIM OF A CLOUD

I reached out
To grasp a cloud,
It remained suspended.

I extended my lips
To kiss a tuft of cloud,
It stayed aloft.

I opened my mouth
To bite a cloud,
My teeth chattered.

With my hands,
I wanted to wrap a cloud
For a dance in the sky.

Just she and I,
But I couldn't find
Her waist.

The wind tossed me
Like a leaf,
And I remained among the clouds.

Broken Dreams

Without a kiss,
Without an embrace,
Without descending to earth,
I remained in the air.

Broken Dreams

A GLOOMY MORNING

In the morning,
When the day begins its journey,
You often feel as if you're
On a cosmic ship
Without hope…
A sleepy pilot
Torments the day,
And it says nothing to you…

By evening,
The ships of your dreams
Come to you,
Empty
Or full…

POETRY EMBRACES YOU

Poetry embraces you,
Like a teardrop resting in your eye...
When the poet departs,
It lingers in the air,
In dreams,
Invisible...
Like a shadow
That measures your stature.
Or the stature seeking its shadow.

Poetry,
Embraces you,
Even when you forget it...

THE KISS

We didn't have time to kiss,
We had time to groan,
Nor to love
Did we have time.
We didn't know how to dance,
We knew how to plow the fields…
And in that timeless time,
The kiss was gossiped about:
He kissed her,
He has kissed her,
She is kissed…
Traps of words
Would ignite and extinguish…
That's why the kiss doesn't kiss us,
Now that we have time to kiss
The coldness of the past
Makes us love more deeply…

THE QUARREL OF THE CLOUDS

Do you see how the clouds quarrel,
And why?
The defiant earth
Orgasms
In velvet hues.

Immersed in mist,
Embracing itself—
Mountains,
Abysses,
Fertile fields,
Burdened with life…

The clouds quarrel,
Pushing,
Tussling in tufts…
They call the rain
To quench the orgasm
That shakes the earth.

LITTLE BIRD

When I was a child,
I wondered,
Little bird,
About you…
Why you had no home…

I wanted to catch you,
To hold you to my chest…

But you flew away,
From branch to branch,
And watched me
With tears in your eyes…

Now, a grown man,
I stand close to you,
And you are not afraid,
And it seems, as then,
You look at me
With tears in your eyes.

Could it be you know
That I am an exile,
Like you were then,
Without a home?!...

SEASONS

I loved the seasons
Without end.
I never understood them,
And I had no one to ask
Why they never came into my life as they were,
Why they never befriended me,
Why they remained suspended like air in the beechwoods
Or like a cloud mixed with raindrops.
The spring of my soul,
In the springtime of my years,
Was withered by the fierce frost of a bitter winter.

The summer of my hairy chest,
In the summer of my years,
Was beaten
By waves from the sea, coming from afar,
From lands filled with the tumult of winter.

I started my autumn
Like a bird fleeing winter,
Not knowing where to end its flight,
A wanderer frightened by the winds.

Broken Dreams

In my late autumn,
I dream of the seasons
That didn't come as I wished.
In a foreign land,
I see them as more languid…

THE DREAM OF FREEDOM

Like a horizon line,
It seems,
It seems,
The dream of freedom...

Like a magic wand, this line
Stirs unknown worlds,
And never stays still...

As you approach,
Another horizon
Beckons you again...

FRIENDS

Two old friends in two villages
Lived apart.

Across a stream on a small footbridge,
They would pass.

With and without occasion,
They invited each other over.

They'd forget to leave,
And night would catch them.

Whenever one would rise
To head home,
The host would say, "I won't let you go alone,"
And would escort him to the old footbridge.

Once they crossed the bridge,
They'd light another pipe,
And the conversation would start anew,
Never ending...

Broken Dreams

Thus, escorting
First one,
Then the other,
They stayed on the bridge
Until morning dawned...

IN LIFE'S SANCTUARY

It's not a train door
On your next journey,
Where you search for a seat
To sit down,

Nor an airplane door
With numbers A, B, C, D, E...

Nor the saddle of a steed
In a running race,
Nor a meadow
Amidst grass and flowers.

It is a long journey,
Fortunate, without return,
To enter life's sanctuary
Without a key,
Only with love.

NIGHTS

Nights grow heavy,
They labor
With hopes,
And seldom give birth
To fresh mornings...

Broken Dreams

WHITE SNOW

Whiteness claims the streets,
Blanketing rooftops,
Boughs weighed down,
Trees adorned with frost,
Mountaintops crowned in white.

Cars wear chains on their tires,
On children's room windows, it paints
Dreams of radiant days to come.

Whiteness drapes everything in sheets,
Even darkness,
Even imperfections it gently lifts.

Humanity rushes to cleanse
The whiteness swiftly,
Yet dirt reappears in the square.

So why do we whiten our teeth,
Why do we make our garments bright white,
And vainly seek white hearts for love?

Broken Dreams

Instead of removing the whiteness
With tractors and bulldozers,
Run to remove the black hatred
That has mercilessly taken its place...

Broken Dreams

WHEN I WAS A BABY

When morning dawned,
Grandmother took the path
To the village mill shop,
With an empty milk bottle,
To stand in line,
For me, her grandchild, newly opened to the world.

My poor mother,
Withered by salty pickles,
Her breasts dry,
Waited for that bottle,
Sorrowful, tears in her eyes.

All too often, the bottle came back empty.

That year,
Many children were born in my village.

RAIN

Whenever life throws me
Rainy days beneath the eaves,
I never
Seek shelter under an umbrella.

Like a keyboard,
Raindrops play melodies,
And I dance in the puddles…

BIRTHPLACE

There,
I followed the river to its source
And learned that the banks
Belong to both me and the river.

There,
I discovered the river
Is never parted from its source,
And far, far away,
It may go, but it never forgets.

There,
I climbed the mountain to its peak,
And the sky kissed my eyes,
And I played with its white cap,
And understood why my grandfather
Pulled his cap down over his brow.

Broken Dreams

THE FIFTH SEASON

In the stumps of the yard,
The broken edges of axes have left,
Like a guestbook,
Endless signatures and lines,
Marks.

The heavy doors of the towers
Cast a breeze,
Like sherbet for brides
When they step over the threshold
For the first time.

In the guest room,
Like a whirlpool,
Magic draws you in.

Everywhere the air embraces,
The springs kiss hands,
Trees open eyes of joy,
Birds scatter clouds and darkness,
Avalanches rest,
Paths widen into trails,
Slopes lend a hand,
Peaks bow before the guest.

Broken Dreams

The four seasons
Change like dancers in a beautiful dance,
But hospitality is a season
That never changes.

OUR ANTIQUITY

It begins in the heights
Where our origins lie.

The mountains stand firm,
They do not move.

Rivers and seas
Are our guests.

They came, embraced the mountains,
Became their limbs.

Broken Dreams

OUR CASTLES

With centuries-old walls,
They sheltered us from storms.
With gentle fingers,
They spun the thread of our path.

In the dried springs of the heart,
Guardians of blessings,
With the sun of our cloudless days.

With white hands,
With white hair,
With white scarves.
Oh, how beautiful,
Our castles stand,
Immortal and serene.

Broken Dreams
THE GRAVE OF THE BORDER

The grave of the border,
Split in two
By the border line,
Inside, some bones
And a skull,
Without a shroud, cast in the mud.

Covered with the same earth
By the hands of states
Without shovels.

Trampled day and night
By nail-studded boots.

One pair at the head,
Another at the feet, row by row.

With a bullet hole in the skull,
Its path of entry and exit,
Sparks flare
In our eyes.

A foggy haze,
A grave with its back
In its belly.

Broken Dreams

No name on the stone,
Birth and death
Without date.

Like rainwater,
Pain and fatigue pour down
On both sides.

MOTHER'S SECRET

Ah, dear mother!
How I wish once more
To be a baby again,
To disturb your sleep,
To see if my mother
Ever truly sleeps.
Do I understand how my mother rests?

As your white hands covered
The embers in the hearth
With ash after midnight,
To rekindle the morning fire anew,
So, too, you hid your sleep
Throughout my life...

WITHOUT POETS

The forest, without poets, breathes air
Without fragrance.

On oak branches, featherless birds
Sing without song.

The oaks, without moss on their trunks,
Do not reveal horizons.

Broken Dreams

THE LAST BITE

The homeland, a bitten apple,
Thrown on the street,
Swarmed by flies devouring its core.
Wanderers push it with a foot,
Lift it, piss on it.
Drunken passersby of the pitch-black night
Spit on it.

When it hung on the branch,
Everyone wanted to reach it,
Throwing stones to rob it,
Tearing it apart
With fierce, blackened teeth.

Broken Dreams

I DIE FOR YOU

I've been dead for a long time.

Flesh with bone,
I keep attached to the body...

But the soul,
No, no.
I have forever given it to beauty...

Broken Dreams

MY YEARS

You'll find them in the rings of the yearning oak,
Returned from endless journeys
Across the dried seas of tears.

Thin lines of sorrow-awaiting
That never came.

Wave upon wave, ring upon ring,
Trembling with lost loves.

In the rings of the oak, springs sleep,
Forgotten winters, wild waves,
Storms with sighs of pain,
Broken branches of hope
Weakened by cruel winds,
By frost and thaw,
Fallen down slopes.

Nights and days
With the rustling lullabies of leaves,
The morning songs of nightingales
With shy glances toward the heights.

Broken Dreams

Spring birds inscribe their songs,
The sounds of love in those lines
Soaring into the blue.

Broken Dreams

SNOW

Snowflakes
Tap on the eyelids.

In your eyes
And in mine...

They bring white dreams
Through the howling wind...

Snow butterflies
Land on our hands.

How afraid we are
To blow on our hands
Lest we kill
These dreamlike butterflies...

But we are distracted,
We remove our scarves,
Our hats,
And reveal our graying hair...

Broken Dreams

Yet for a few moments,
We forget them
In the magical
Dreamlike
Snow...

THE FIRST KISS

Forgotten by lovers on the shore,
Tides and waves toss it with their horns,
White foam takes selfies with it,
Songbirds on the rail chirp unwittingly,
Sinking it into the blue.

Morning rays find it
On the calm waves,
Like a seagull,
Oh, how sweet it was!

Broken Dreams

HOPES

Nights lean
On the moon's shoulders,
Happily awaiting mornings.
They dew dreams
With the sun's gaze.

THE SEA OF POETRY

At the sea's edge,
The tide rolls in
And the ebb retreats
Relentlessly...

Like a repentant verse
Exchanging
A cherished line...

The foam of waves
Speaks of struggle
In its confession.

ETERNAL LOVE

The shirt on the body,
The shoes,
And the journeys,
Are but temporary...

Sorrows,
Joys,
And bank accounts,
Remain just as
Ephemeral...

But what endures, truly ours?
Eternal love...

ABANDONED OAK

Amidst its branches,
I read the clouds
Like the lines on my palms...

Drowsiness overtakes me...

I wake within its shade,
Wrapping around my own,
Under this oak.

With roots deep in the earth,
The oak remained,
Through hail, snow, and rain.
And I journeyed,
Like a shaken tree,
To other places,
Planting roots...

Now my thoughts dwell
On that oak,
The summer bird flown far,
Leaving an abandoned nest
In its trunk...

Broken Dreams

In that hollow, and in me,
I smoke my autumn in solitude.

Where do you go, oh summer bird?
I wonder, though migration suits you...

The migration of people
Brings deeper sorrow...

ARTISTS

Some artists embellish their work
With stolen crystals
And see themselves as beautiful...

They chase a rhythm
For their abyssal hearts,
To adorn themselves...
And others.

But true artists
Give away
Their abundant selves,
Beautifying the world

Broken Dreams
I WANT TO PUT SLEEP TO SLEEP

Crumbs of the homeland
Carried by birds each morning
Land on the shattered glass of memories.
A little more, a little more,
Sleep-drunkenness lingers.

Sun rays
On my eyelids
Whisper,
Speak,
Disrupting
The sleep
That closes my eyes.

All say,
"Blessed is he who died in his sleep!"

Ah, may your mouth dry up,
My homeland, never.
Both dead and alive,
We stay awake...

Broken Dreams
I CARRY MY TEAR EVERYWHERE

I carry my tear everywhere,
Hidden in my eyes,
No one can find it.
Drop by drop, it moistens the song of my words.
I can give everything,
But not that,
Never!
Even on the last day, I won't give it,
Let it dry
With my eyes...

Broken Dreams

NOW I AM FAR AWAY

I quench my thirst
By drinking my dreams.

Yet still,
The thirst grows.

And so does the hunger
For days that stretch
Endlessly,
In waiting,
To return
To the homeland...

But the allure
Of the dream
Lulls me,
Sun rays
On my eyelids
Extend
Spears of longing
That pierce
The balloons of futile waiting...

Broken Dreams

I am far away,
I know,
But dreams like these
Sustain my life,
Give me love,
And to hope,
Youth.

INSPECTION

I cross borders,
Airports,
Cars,
Sniffer dogs...
Where am I going?

Memory, like a fiery membrane,
Wraps the moments
I leave behind...

No inspection
Happens there,
It ignites my steps
To reach home, in a foreign land...

Memory calms
Perhaps because I could never restrain it.
For this tear,
I have evidence...

Broken Dreams

DAYS

Years forgot to set forth on the path of light,
Nights turned to darkness, devouring the Moon.

Monuments—
Faces stripped of shine.

Days of the week stretch in colorless gowns,
Blooming without bloom at dawn...

DESOLATE FOREST

The roses are without bloom,
The trees without scent,
The barren nights
Have consumed the Moon,
Leaving its shadow
In the dim mirror
Of a forgotten pond...

Desolate forest,
Trees like candles,
Lit
By a waning star...

Through them, I see
The smoke of days...

Here, memory hangs
On bare branches
After the storms,
As in all ages,
Leaving the trees
With shadows of worries...

Broken Dreams

THAT MORNING…

That morning,
The phone vibrated,
While I lay with eyes closed,
Stretched out
In the silent whirlpool
Of solitude…

A heartbeat's pulse
Pressed a finger
On the button of memory.

The whirlpool of solitude
Was emptied
By regret.

Like someone drowning
In loneliness,
I emerged.

From afar,
Flocks of
Birds of longing
Approached.

Broken Dreams

Like rays to hearts,
The message
In those letters
Brought your scent—
As if it were steam,
Softly enveloping
The phone screen…

You had wept
So far
And yet so near,
Though across the ocean…

Broken Dreams

HOW OFTEN...

A stone tumbled into the beech forest,
Shattered on the trees,
Scattered in pieces.
In haste and without time,
The leaves of the beeches
Burst into tears.

Like an autumn moon
In its descent,
That stone fell...
A lament
For not being set into a wall.

Long ago, the beech branches
Extended their arms,
Awaiting the leaves
That struggled to grow on them...

How often, O Lord,
Does fate strike us
When we least expect it,
When we are unaware...

FAMILY DAY

Seven days a week,
Too few for the poor,
Too many for the rich.

I want to add one more day,
A day for family,
Between Sunday
And Saturday.

Wealth and poverty
In balance would stay,
So we can discern
Each one's boundary…

MY VERSE

I hang letters on the moon's rays,
Stir them in the soul of the seas,
In darkness and light,
In light and darkness,
As I trace each day
The tears of those
Who fled from you, homeland...

The sky with its blue throat,
The sky that keeps rainbow colors,
Teaches its birds
Never to forget their nest...

My verse becomes a blade of grass
For the nest,
My verse becomes years of longing
Like waves
That beat and speak
To the shores of departures.

And it vents the thunder of sorrows
Where every tear dries
In the sun of hope...

TRAIN STATION

The train's sirens scream,
Drowned in the ears
Of the vast space.

Open,
Close,
The train doors
At stations...
Hugs,
Kisses,
Cries—
They do not scream...

But the train carries them,
And screams with them,
For the days like trains
Loaded with sorrows,
Racing towards stations
Without names...

NOBODY KNOWS US

In the desert of tears
Nobody knows us.

Like birds on a map of the globe,
We search for a nest,
Without shelter,
Without documents,
Sometimes just numbers,
A thousand,
A million.

Like a bird flapping its wings,
Our fate struggles.

We dig into the soil of faith
To plant a seed,
Somewhere in a corner of freedom
To stay.

But nobody knows us,
When we are without you,
Homeland.

Broken Dreams
THROUGH THE LIGHT OF PAIN

Soaked from the rain,
Saturated with bitterness,
Without a roof over his head
In the icy city
With dazzling lights,
A poet wanders…

Buildings with glass like screens
Shine,
As trucks dump leftover food
Into bins…

This consumerist world
Throws away
Humanity there.

A beggar
Extends his hand,
Another
Collects scraps
From the bins…

Broken Dreams

On icy streets
Shelters freeze,
Only the poet's compassion
Perhaps can thaw them…

Glass windows shine
With advertisements of all kinds.

No light,
More than the light of pain,
Blinded the poet
More than any other light…

Broken Dreams

POLAR BEAR

I don't want to see the leaf
As it falls.

But the tree
In full leaf,
I do.

And when the snowflakes fall,
I don't want to see them.

Only when they melt,
Their sight warms me...

Nor the sky when it's frowning,
Just without clouds.

The cold numbs me,
But the song's echo
Thaws me.

Tell me when they arrive.

All of these
Take away my hunger...

THE BOSOM OF THE EARTH

In the bosom of the earth,
So many thirsty dawns
Drink.

With dry lips and smiles,
The dawns…
For the bosom of the earth never dries,
But often turns bitter
Where deceitful man drinks,
The anti-man…

Broken Dreams
CONTRAST OF EMIGRANTS

In the belly of the plane, like for a basketball game,
We boarded then with noise, far from our homeland,
Innocent sinners
Of departure.

We took with us the shouts,
The pushes, and the drunkenness of time,
There in the soft seats
Our entire geography crumbled.

Cities,
Neighborhoods, and villages in sequence
Became numbers and letters: a, b, c, d.
With the noise of the plane's takeoff
Laughter and hope mingled.

The plane windows sweated from the steam of dry mouths,
From interview words at embassies,
The plane roared
Like a chorus of fans at a winning match,
With laughter, taunts, and handshakes...

In small notebooks, new addresses were noted,
Names and phone numbers that were never called.

Broken Dreams

Now, after 25 or 30 years,
The boys and girls of yesterday
Return in the plane's belly without noise.

Heads bowed and with wrinkles on their foreheads and cheeks,
With tired eyes,
Some pushed in wheelchairs,
Others holding canes.

Silence does not compete with the engine's roar,
Seats with numbers a, b, c, d
Contain the whole world.

Now without noise, the windows are without steam,
The few words of nearly 30 years
Are not heard,
Words remain dead
On lips,
After the game is lost,
The hoarse fans
Have no strength for beers,
They return,
Return as quickly as possible
To lie down and sleep...

THE BIRD'S LAMENT

My oak shed its leaves,
Its branches withered,
The trunk shriveled,
Like an old grandfather.

In its final days,
In the feverish glow of slumber,
The bird, its old friend,
Who nested there,
Came and wept
For the oak's moan.
It could no longer see the sky
Because of the tears that sprouted
In its eyes,
And the stone in its tiny chest
Silenced its song...

Broken Dreams
THE BALLAD OF DEPARTURE

Our earth cracks
From tears that never dry.

Flowers wait
To be watered
By our hands,
With dreams,
With memories
As old
As the world.

But they
Do not bring rain,
Even though the shores
Fill with pebbles.

Without us,
Our footprints,
In the absence of steps,
Disappear.

But our voices,
Where are our voices?

Broken Dreams

Did the earth hide them
Inside,
For a volcano?

A day will come,
(May that day never come!)
From our departure
On a gloomy morning,
Even on the last stone
We will not find a name
Carved.

The cracking earth
Waits for our rain of longing
To water it…

In that alone, I believe…

TRINITY

Our language is a mother—
Does a mother have an age?

An old mother,
With her, the language.

The first babble,
The bud of life.

All flowers,
Crowns of glory,
Grow from this bud.

Language, a divine blessing,
Mother, a blessing of the soul…

Which birthed the other?

Mother first,
Language second,
And the homeland,
A creation of mother
And language—
A trinity…

Broken Dreams

HANDS

Golden when they build bridges
That link shores.
In operating rooms,
When they remove tumors
Or mend broken ribs.

Blessed
When they water flowers,
Raise
Children.

Tainted
In wicked deeds.

For the mute,
They are a miracle.

For applause that wounds,
Why did you give us two, O God?

Broken Dreams
FORGIVE ME, MY POETRY

Today, on Book Day,
I speak to poetry:

How often we hurt you, dear,
Sometimes,
Throwing you on shelves
Like household items.

You are not like a sheep
We milk in the pen.
You are a wild pearl,
A chestnut burr,
To grasp your essence,
We must bloody our hands.

Sometimes morning dew,
Sometimes the scorching sun,
A burning song
For a hungry soul,
You cannot be confined
Like an hour of the day.
You refuse a cage,
Like air, you are
Poetry...

LIFE IS A MOTHER

The earth, without a mother,
Would be barren.

The world,
No matter how vast,
Seeks a mother to hold it,
And finds her, and loses her,
Again and again,
In the word "brotherhood,"
Nation to nation,
State to state...

Broken Dreams

MY AUNT'S PASSPORT

My aunt's house clung to the border,
On the other side, her elderly mother,
Was my grandmother.

The bells of the rams echoed on both sides,
Their grazing land split by a line.

Drums and tambourines resounded
At weddings or henna nights.

On one side, my grandmother wept,
On the other, her daughter cried,
My poor aunt.

Fifty years with the pyramid
In between.

The border was removed,
At her mother's grave,
A tear falls from my aunt's eye...

Broken Dreams

AM I A HOMELAND?

If I am not,
May I never be born!

If I am not,
And have been born,
May I never grow up!

If I am not,
And have grown,
May I never age!

If I am not,
And have aged,
May death come bitterly to me!

If I am not,
And have died,
May I never find a grave!

MORNING COFFEE MUSIC

Morning awakens with coffee
And music,
Sweet music,
Soothing and enticing.
The river flows
With multicolored flora
And endless blue.
Am I drinking coffee
Or blueness?!
The river flows
Through my veins…

THE DAM

The river's wildness halts,
Its waves softened,
Like a battered bull,
Resting its head
On the dam's pillow.

There it slumbers,
The banks unshaken,
Turbines send forth light.

Even the soul needs
Such a dam...

THE SMILE OF TOMORROW

The sun shone brightly,
Filling the house with light.
The newborn begins
A new castle
With a golden foundation stone,
The smile of tomorrow
Radiating with light...

MY STORY

In my grandson,
With eyes like the sky,
Warmed by the sun,
My story begins,
For he inherits
The lineage of our kin...

Broken Dreams

MOTHERS

A mother draws her child from her breast
Only when she's on horseback,
On a steep slope,
At the edge of an abyss,
Crossing a wild stream.
She lifts the cradle from her lap
And hands it to her husband
For safety...
More than hunger,
She fears for his life...

Broken Dreams

PARALLELS

Raindrops find their path,
Streams rush
Like wild rams,
Pushing stones
Downward
Into ravines.
They tear at slopes,
Hurling like cudgels
Through briars and beeches.
Roots
And trunks of oaks
Collide.
Hailstones crackle
On rooftops,
On rocks,
Cows and sheep gather in clearings,
Beneath any nearby rock shelter,
Or around a pine trunk,
Silent,
Heads bowed.
They resemble gatherings
At funerals
Or dirty political rallies.

SHORT LITERARY BIOGRAPHY

SAMI MULAJ

was born in Tropojë (Old Tropojë), Albania. He completed his secondary education at the "Asim Vokshi" General High School in Bajram Curri. From 1976 to 1981, he pursued higher education at the University of Tirana, where he graduated from the Faculty of Geology and Mining, specializing in mining and mineral enrichment.

Mulaj worked as a mining engineer in the chromium and quartz mines of the Tropojë district and in the coal mine in Gërdec, located in the Tirana district.

He has had a long-standing collaboration with various periodicals, both in Albania and the United States. From a young age, Mulaj published writings on a range of social and political topics in numerous publications, including Zëri i Rinisë (The Voice of Youth), Bashkimi (The Unity), Zëri i Popullit (The Voice of the People), Gazeta Studenti (The Studenti Newspaper), Gazeta Shkëlzeni (The Shkëlzeni Newspaper), Gazeta Kosova (The Kosovo Newspaper), Rilindja Demokratike (The Democratic Rebirth), Gazeta e Alpeve (The Alps Newspaper), VOAL in Switzerland, Bota Sot (The World Today), GazetaIllyria (The Illyria Newspaper), and Dielli (The Sun) in New York.

Since 1997, he has lived in New Jersey, USA. He is married and has two sons and two grandchildren.

Broken Dreams

Mulaj is deeply involved in the patriotic and nationalistic circles of the Albanian-American community. He is a respected and beloved voice, consistently engaged with the concerns of the homeland and Albanian territories.

He has published four books of poetry: Lisat e Mi të Diellit (My Sunlit Trees), Buzëqeshja e së Nesërmes (The Smile of Tomorrow), Dy Anadrinët (The Two Opposite Drin Riversides), and Stina e Pestë (The Fifth Season), as well as a collection of short stories entitled Gurët që Pikojnë Dhimbje (The Stones that Weep with Pain), all of which have been well-received by readers and literary critics.

Printed in Great Britain
by Amazon